PSYCHICS

BY LILY LOYE

APEX

WWW.APEXEDITIONS.COM

Apex is distributed by North Star Editions:
sales@northstareditions.com | 888-417-0195

Produced for Apex by Red Line Editorial.

Photographs ©: Shutterstock Images, cover, 1, 4–5, 6–7, 8, 9, 10–11, 12–13, 14, 16–17, 18, 20–21, 22–23, 24–25, 26–27, 29; iStockphoto, 15; N. Currier/Library of Congress, 19

Library of Congress Control Number: 2021915673

ISBN
978-1-63738-164-9 (hardcover)
978-1-63738-200-4 (paperback)
978-1-63738-269-1 (ebook pdf)
978-1-63738-236-3 (hosted ebook)

Printed in the United States of America
Mankato, MN
012022

NOTE TO PARENTS AND EDUCATORS

Apex books are designed to build literacy skills in striving readers. Exciting, high-interest content attracts and holds readers' attention. The text is carefully leveled to allow students to achieve success quickly. Additional features, such as bolded glossary words for difficult terms, help build comprehension.

TABLE OF CONTENTS

CHAPTER 1

MESSAGE FROM BEYOND

A man stands in front of a crowd. He closes his eyes. "I'm getting a J name," he says. A woman gasps. "My husband, Jason, died last year," she says.

Some psychics perform in shows where they attempt to read people's minds.

"Jason, yes," says the man. "He's here with me now. He wants you to know how much he loves you. He wants you to be happy."

Some psychics do individual readings. Others use their skills for groups of people.

People may visit psychics to hear from loved ones who have died.

7

Psychics often make general predictions. But listeners feel like the words are just for them.

The woman's eyes fill with tears. The crowd claps, and the man bows.

HIRING A PSYCHIC

Some psychics work at shops or fairs. Visitors pay them to use their skills. Fortune-tellers make **predictions** or answer questions. Palm readers also tell the future. They look at lines on people's hands.

Some psychics use tarot cards. The pictures on the cards have different meanings.

CHAPTER 2

WHAT ARE PSYCHICS?

Psychics claim to have **supernatural** abilities. They sense things other people cannot. These powers are called extrasensory perception (ESP).

Some psychics say information comes to them in dreams. Others say they have help from spirits.

People may visit a fortune-teller to ask questions about what they should do.

ESP includes several abilities. Some psychics sense the future. They may see events before they happen. They may give people warnings or advice.

About two in five people in the United States believe in ESP.

Some psychics **communicate** with spirits. Others use **telepathy**. They may read people's minds. Or they may send messages through thoughts.

Psychics sometimes close their eyes or touch their heads. They say this helps them focus.

Communicating with spirits is called channeling.

Pet psychics claim to know the thoughts of animals.

MEDIUMS

Mediums try to contact people who have died. Some mediums hear spirits. They tell others what the spirits say. Other mediums go into **trances**. They let spirits take over their bodies.

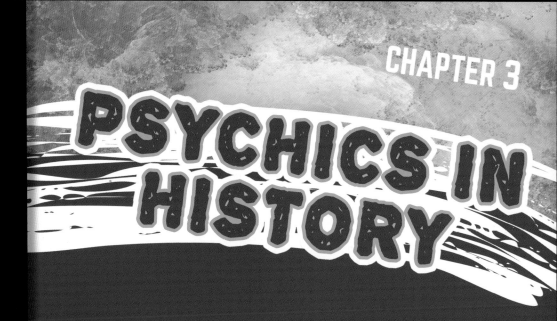

CHAPTER 3

PSYCHICS IN HISTORY

People have tried to predict the future and contact the dead since **ancient** times. Many kingdoms had fortune-tellers. Greece and Egypt were two examples.

Fortune-tellers sometimes use crystal balls, candles, or other tools to help them see the future.

In the mid-1800s, a religion called spiritualism became very popular. It involved contacting the dead. **Séances** and mediums played a big role.

At a séance, people often sit at a table in the dark and hold hands.

Maggie (left) and Kate (center) Fox first reported hearing ghosts when they were young girls.

TALKING WITH GHOSTS

Maggie and Kate Fox were famous psychics. They lived in the 1800s. The sisters claimed to talk to ghosts. They said the ghosts made knocking sounds to send messages.

Today, some psychics post predictions or videos on the internet.

By the late 1900s, psychics appeared on TV. They showed off their skills. Some had huge numbers of followers.

Some famous scientists believed in ESP. One was Thomas Edison.

CHAPTER 4

JUST A TRICK?

Many psychics are fakes. They use a variety of tricks. Some psychics research their **clients**. Then they pretend to sense this information.

Some psychics trick people to make money. Famous psychics can earn millions of dollars.

Psychics may also guess information. They often start by saying something general. Then they watch people closely. They use people's words and body language to guess what to say next.

GOOD GUESSING

If a guess seems right, psychics say more about it. If it seems wrong, they try something else. People tend to remember the correct guesses more than the wrong ones.

Using signals from people to make guesses about them is called cold reading.

However, not all ESP can be explained by these tricks. So, some scientists study ESP. They hope to learn more.

Some people try to use ESP to find missing people.

To study ESP, scientists often have people guess what's on cards they can't see.

COMPREHENSION QUESTIONS

Write your answers on a separate piece of paper.

1. Write a sentence explaining one ability a person with ESP might have.

2. Would you want to be able to read people's minds? Why or why not?

3. When did the religion of spiritualism become very popular?

> A. in the mid-1800s
> B. in the late 1900s
> C. in ancient times

4. How would watching someone's body language help a psychic know what to say?

> A. A psychic could read the person's mind.
> B. A psychic could guess if her comment was on the right track.
> C. A psychic could hear from spirits in the room.

5. What does **research** mean in this book?

*Some psychics **research** their clients. Then they pretend to sense this information.*

    A. to find information about someone
    B. to pay money to someone
    C. to tell lies about someone

6. What does **contact** mean in this book?

*Mediums try to **contact** people who have died. Some mediums hear spirits. They tell others what the spirits say.*

    A. to slap or hit
    B. to talk with
    C. to chase away

Answer key on page 32.

GLOSSARY

ancient
Very old or from long ago.

clients
People who hire someone to do work for them.

communicate
To send and receive messages.

predictions
Statements about what will happen in the future.

readings
Times when psychics use their abilities to tell people information.

séances
Meetings where people try to contact the dead.

supernatural
Outside the usual things that can be explained by science.

telepathy
The ability to communicate by thinking, or to know the thoughts of others.

trances
States where people aren't aware of what's happening around them.

TO LEARN MORE

BOOKS

Borgert-Spaniol, Megan. *ESP: Does a Sixth Sense Exist?* Minneapolis: Abdo Publishing, 2019.

Cronin, G. L. *Psychic Powers*. Vero Beach, FL: Rourke Educational Media, 2019.

Polinsky, Paige V. *ESP*. Minneapolis: Bellwether Media, 2020.

ONLINE RESOURCES

Visit **www.apexeditions.com** to find links and resources related to this title.

ABOUT THE AUTHOR

Lily Loye has been an editor and children's book author for more than 20 years. She loves all things scary, spooky, and creepy but has never seen a ghost herself. She lives in Mankato, Minnesota, with her family, plus two dogs, one cat, and a cuddly bearded dragon.

INDEX

Answer Key:
1. Answers will vary; **2.** Answers will vary; **3.** A; **4.** B; **5.** A; **6.** B